ALA Survey of Librarian Salaries 1996

Mary Jo Lynch, *Project Director*

ALA Survey Report

American Library Association
Office for Research and Statistics

American Library Association
Chicago and London 1996

ISBN: 0-8389-7841-X
ISSN: 0747-7201

Copyright © 1996 by the American Library Association.
All rights reserved except those which may be granted by Sections 107
and 108 of the Copyright Revision Act of 1976.

Printed in the United States of America.

Acknowledgments

Thanks are due to the many respondents who completed our questionnaires. Without their cooperation, this report would not be possible. We are grateful to the Association of Research Libraries (ARL) for sharing data with us as described in Appendix D and especially to Martha Kyrillidou, ARL Program Officer for Statistics and Measurement who sent the data electronically. We are also grateful to Ed Lakner, Diane La Barbera, Jian Qin, Leah Myers and other staff at the Library Research Center of the Graduate School of Library and Information Science at the University of Illinois who managed the mailings and processed the returns. Appendix A was prepared by Maxine Moore, Administrative Assistant in ALA's Office for Library Personnel Resources (OLPR). Appendix B and C were prepared by Renée Prestegard, Associate Director and Librarian in ALA's Library and Research Center (LARC). Finally, thanks are due to Kimberly Dewis Administrative Assistant in the Office for Research and Statistics (ORS) for word processing the revised text and tables.

This is the first time, since the series began in 1992, that Margaret Myers has not been involved in this survey. Margaret, former Director of OLPR, took early retirement from ALA in October 1995 and shortly thereafter began a two year assignment with the Peace Corps in Botswana. Margaret was instrumental in starting this series of surveys and participated fully in solving problems that occurred over the years. We missed her presence this year and dedicate this report to her.

Table of Contents

Acknowledgments

Introduction   1

Results   3

    Director   4
    Deputy/Associate/Assistant Director   7
    Department Head/Branch Head   10
    Reference/Information Librarian   13
    Cataloger and/or Classifier   16

    Children's and/or Young Adult Services Librarian   19
    Beginning Librarian   21

Discussion

    Summary of Results   25
        Salaries by Position   25
        Salaries by Type of Library   26
        Salaries by Region of the U.S.   26

    Complicating Factors   27
        Meaning of "Full-Time"   27
        Meaning of "Professional"   27
        Salaries Below $20,000   28
        Job Levels or Faculty Ranks   28
        Longevity Pay   28

    Level of Experience   28

Appendixes

    A. Compensation Surveys Providing Information on Library Workers   29
    B. ALA Policies Relating to Compensation Issues   37
    C. Selected Bibliography on Compensation and Benefits   41
    D. Technical Considerations   43
    E. Cover Letter   49
    F. Survey Questionnaire   51
    G. Salaries Paid for Less than a 12-month Year in Academic Libraries   55

Introduction

Librarians, the people who hire them, and interested others often ask the American Library Association (ALA) Office for Library Personnel Resources (OLPR) to tell them what salary might be paid to a librarian in a particular position, working in a particular type of library, in a particular part of the U.S. To fill the need for information of this kind, ALA began conducting a periodic survey of salaries for full-time professionals in academic and public libraries. Reports were published biennially from 1982 to 1988 and became annual in 1989.

This report, the twelfth in a series, presents salaries paid to incumbents in six positions commonly found in U.S. academic and public libraries. Salaries were reported as of April 1, 1996. For each of five positions, the report contains six tables, one for each of five library types and one for all five combined. The sixth position--children's and/or young adult services librarian--is shown only for public libraries. Each of the tables shows the range, mean, first quartile, median, and third quartile of salaries in four geographic regions. Salaries paid to beginning professionals are also displayed in the same way.

The 1996 report shares the following characteristics with its immediate predecessor:

- It is based on a survey of **libraries**, not individual librarians.

- It is based on a survey of **full-time** positions.

- It is based on a survey of **public and academic** libraries only. (Sources for salaries in other libraries are given in Appendix A.)

- The public and academic library universe is stratified by the same **type/size criteria**: public libraries serving populations of from 25,000 to 99,999, public libraries serving populations of 100,000 or more, two-year colleges, four-year colleges, and universities. (The last category includes all institutions offering work beyond the bachelor's level).

- The nation is stratified into the same **geographic areas**: North Atlantic, Great Lakes and Plains, Southeast, West and Southwest (see Appendix D for list of states).

- It shows the **first quartile, median, and third quartile** for salaries paid in each type/size of library and region in addition to the **mean and range** (low and high) for each position reported.

- It shows salaries paid to staff **with master's degrees from programs in library and information studies accredited by ALA**.

- It shows salaries for **beginning librarians** in both public and academic libraries.

- It shows salaries for **five positions in both public and academic libraries** (Director, Deputy/Associate/Assistant Director, Department Head/Branch Head, Reference/Information Librarian, Cataloger and/or Classifier), and **one position in public libraries only** (Children's and/or Young Adult Services Librarian).

The 1996 survey also contained three questions asked on a one-time-only basis in order to gather data needed to plan improvements in the report and its distribution:

1a.   Does your library have the *ALA Survey of Libraries Salaries, 1995?*

   _____ Yes (Skip to 2a)
   _____ No
   _____ Don't Know (Skip to 3)

   1b. Why do you not have a copy? (Check all that apply and skip to 3)

   _____ Did not know about it
   _____ Can't afford it
   _____ Don't need it

2a.   Have you used a copy in the last twelve months?

   _____ Yes
   _____ No (Skip to 3)

   2b. How did it help you? (Check all that apply)

   _____ Setting salaries for a new position
   _____ Bargaining for increase in salary for my staff
   _____ Bargaining for increase in salary for myself
   _____ Other (please specify)

3.   Please comment on how ALA could provide more useful information on librarian salaries.

The Library Research Center of the University of Illinois Graduate School of Library and Information Science performed the mailing, processing, and computer analysis of the questionnaires. Mary Jo Lynch, Director of ALA's Office for Research and Statistics (ORS), directed the project and wrote this report.

We hope the results of the survey will be useful to employers of librarians who need this information in administering an equitable pay plan and to librarians seeking employment or career advancement.

Results

The survey questionnaire was mailed to 1,278 randomly selected libraries on March 31, 1996. Samples were drawn from twenty groups of libraries formed by stratifying five type-of-library categories by four regions of the U. S. Appendix D describes how groups were formed and sampled. By the second week in June, useable responses had been received from 966 libraries, 75.6 percent of those sampled.

The results of this survey are presented on the following pages in seven sets of tables. The first five sets present salaries paid to incumbents in positions common to both public and academic libraries. Respondents were asked to report all full-time incumbents *with master's degrees from programs in library and information studies accredited by ALA* except for beginning professionals, whose salaries are shown in a special table. There are three pages of tables for each position. The first table presents salaries paid in medium-sized public libraries, i.e., those serving between 25,000 and 99,999. For each of four regions of the country and for the nation as a whole, the table shows the number of positions reported (N), the lowest salary and the highest salary (range), the mean (arithmetic average), the first quartile, median, and third quartile. This pattern is repeated for large public libraries (i.e., those serving populations of 100,000 or more), and for libraries in two-year colleges, four-year colleges, and in universities (i.e., institutions offering work beyond the baccalaureate degree).

Following these five sets of tables is a smaller set for children's and/or young adult services librarian. For this position, tables are given only for the two sizes of public libraries and for all public libraries.

The last set of tables describes salaries paid to beginning professionals following the pattern set in the first six sets of tables.

The following example illustrates how to interpret the tables. In the first table for the position of director--the table presenting salaries paid in medium-sized public libraries--there were 92 salaries reported from the North Atlantic region. The lowest of these was $28,285 and the highest was $104,000. When all the salaries were added together and the result was divided by the total number (92) the average or mean was $57,621. When all the salaries were arrayed from low to high, 25 percent of them fell below $45,865, the first quartile, 50 percent fell below $54,322, the median, and 50 percent were above $54,322. Seventy-five percent fell below $67,691, the third quartile, and 25 percent were above that amount. The middle 50 percent of the salaries fell between $45,865 and $67,691.

Two caveats should be observed in reading the tables. The higher the number of cases (N), the more reliable the results of the sample in giving a true picture of the total population. When the number of cases is less than twenty-five, the results should be used with caution. This caution is especially applicable to the regional data for libraries where the number of professional staff is often small--medium sized public libraries, four-year colleges, and two-year colleges. Another caveat is that when the mean and the median are not close together, the mean is being influenced by some unusual values. When the mean is much higher than the median, there are several very high salaries. When the mean is much lower than the median, there are several very low salaries.

Director
(Page 1 of 3)

Chief administrative officer of the library or library system. Plans and directs all aspects of the operation. May have job title such as Librarian or Head Librarian.

Medium-sized Public Library
(Serving a population of from 25,000 to 99,999)

	MEAN	FIRST QUARTILE	MEDIAN	THIRD QUARTILE
North Atlantic N=92 Range= $28,255-$104,000	57,621	45,865	54,322	67,691
Great Lakes & Plains N=95 Range= $27,430-$83,636	51,038	42,289	48,168	57,800
Southeast N=49 Range= $24,493-$61,859	43,029	37,750	42,448	49,088
West & Southwest N=55 Range= $30,500-$89,244	51,859	40,392	48,844	60,828
All Regions N=291 Range= $24,493-$104,000	51,926	42,000	48,967	60,081

Large Public Library
(Serving a population of 100,000 or more)

	MEAN	FIRST QUARTILE	MEDIAN	THIRD QUARTILE
North Atlantic N=31 Range= $38,000-$137,500	75,466	61,282	78,000	90,000
Great Lakes & Plains N=35 Range= $39,956-$108,420	75,952	60,986	76,274	92,000
Southeast N=48 Range= $41,653-$105,336	66,544	52,079	65,399	80,459
West & Southwest N=56 Range= $34,800-$123,561	74,839	63,027	78,951	85,503
All Regions N=170 Range= $34,800-$137,500	72,840	57,100	72,898	85,790

SOURCE: ALA SURVEY OF LIBRARIAN SALARIES, 1996

Director (Page 2 of 3)

Chief administrative officer of the library or library system. Plans and directs all aspects of the operation. May have job title such as Librarian or Head Librarian.

Two-Year College

	MEAN	FIRST QUARTILE	MEDIAN	THIRD QUARTILE
North Atlantic N=33 Range=$38,605-$73,000	55,892	47,011	56,884	62,615
Great Lakes & Plains N=29 Range=$30,000-$79,721	50,933	40,000	51,206	58,000
Southeast N=35 Range= $24,000-$71,176	45,975	40,800	46,559	52,457
West & Southwest N=34 Range= $22,386-$74,597	49,397	44,000	50,200	54,600
All Regions N=131 Range= $22,386-$79,721	50,459	43,000	51,068	57,419

Four-Year College

	MEAN	FIRST QUARTILE	MEDIAN	THIRD QUARTILE
North Atlantic N=33 Range=$29,100-$84,500	52,426	41,000	50,000	65,000
Great Lakes & Plains N=31 Range=$27,250-$63,039	44,521	36,758	46,000	52,212
Southeast N=30 Range=$25,000-$70,800	41,403	34,620	39,100	46,500
West & Southwest N=19 Range=$24,000-$88,602	47,660	35,000	43,776	58,120
All Regions N=113 Range= $24,000-$88,602	46,530	36,400	43,668	55,600

SOURCE: ALA SURVEY OF LIBRARIAN SALARIES, 1996

Director (Page 3 of 3)

Chief administrative officer of the library or library system. Plans and directs all aspects of the operation. May have job title such as Librarian or Head Librarian.

University

	MEAN	FIRST QUARTILE	MEDIAN	THIRD QUARTILE
North Atlantic N=60 Range=$35,464-$170,000	70,106	49,577	64,575	77,016
Great Lakes & Plains N=54 Range=$30,400-$120,650	60,760	42,000	57,250	73,500
Southeast N=50 Range=$27,560-$169,200	65,662	44,000	62,318	75,000
West & Southwest N=52 Range=$27,300-$120,060	68,458	54,570	65,617	85,250
All Regions N=216 Range=$27,300-$170,000	66,344	47,153	62,318	77,207

All Academic and Public Libraries

	MEAN	FIRST QUARTILE	MEDIAN	THIRD QUARTILE
North Atlantic N=249 Range=$28,255-$170,000	61,934	46,968	58,677	71,150
Great Lakes & Plains N=244 Range=$27,250-$120,650	55,923	42,174	52,262	64,539
Southeast N=212 Range=$24,000-$169,200	53,947	40,744	49,353	62,318
West & Southwest N=216 Range=$22,386-$123,561	61,056	45,100	58,371	74,810
All Regions N=921 Range=$22,386-$170,000	58,297	43,460	54,038	68,625

SOURCE: ALA SURVEY OF LIBRARIAN SALARIES, 1996

Deputy/Associate/Assistant Director

(Page 1 of 3)

Aids Director in planning and directing some or all aspects of library or library system. May manage a major aspect of the library operation (e.g., technical services, public services, collection development, systems/automation).

Medium-sized Public Library
(Serving a population of from 25,000 to 99,999)

	MEAN	FIRST QUARTILE	MEDIAN	THIRD QUARTILE
North Atlantic N=58 Range=$28,392-$77,501	48,249	38,181	49,378	55,680
Great Lakes & Plains N=47 Range=$21,900-$54,760	39,070	32,983	39,527	45,990
Southeast N=26 Range=$23,695-$50,458	36,000	30,000	36,392	41,298
West & Southwest N=24 Range=$26,500-$52,728	38,695	32,677	39,410	45,255
All Regions N=155 Range=$21,900-$77,501	41,932	33,519	41,184	50,137

Large Public Library
(Serving a population of 100,000 or more)

	MEAN	FIRST QUARTILE	MEDIAN	THIRD QUARTILE
North Atlantic N=87 Range=$36,333-$126,980	63,855	53,044	62,689	72,748
Great Lakes & Plains N=42 Range=$28,040-$102,792	60,115	46,200	65,048	71,878
Southeast N=90 Range=$27,997-$80,904	51,506	43,635	51,351	59,827
West & Southwest N=102 Range=$26,448-$104,588	56,795	46,820	55,536	64,776
All Regions N=321 Range=$26,448-$126,980	57,660	46,883	56,737	66,900

SOURCE: ALA SURVEY OF LIBRARIAN SALARIES, 1996

Deputy/Associate/Assistant Director (Page 2 of 3)

Aids Director in planning and directing some or all aspects of library or library system. May manage a major aspect of the library operation (e.g., technical services, public services, collection development, systems/automation).

Two-Year College

	MEAN	FIRST QUARTILE	MEDIAN	THIRD QUARTILE
North Atlantic N=13 Range=$25,809-$72,079	47,184	35,380	47,637	55,251
Great Lakes & Plains N=8 Range=$27,000-$67,791	43,749	32,907	42,693	52,000
Southeast N=12 Range=$24,000-$53,183	37,082	28,682	39,321	40,502
West & Southwest N=12 Range=$23,000-$61,753	40,965	31,156	37,966	53,976
All Regions N=45 Range=$23,000-$72,079	42,221	32,000	39,931	52,000

Four-Year College

	MEAN	FIRST QUARTILE	MEDIAN	THIRD QUARTILE
North Atlantic N=15 Range=$27,288-$65,100	43,979	36,000	42,979	47,250
Great Lakes & Plains N=15 Range=$22,000-$44,000	34,357	28,500	36,000	40,572
Southeast N=13 Range=$23,000-$49,307	35,253	31,000	35,700	39,000
West & Southwest N=9 Range=$27,000-$67,464	41,153	32,535	35,544	40,600
All Regions N=52 Range=$22,000-$67,464	38,533	32,648	36,380	42,990

Deputy/Associate/Assistant Director (Page 3 of 3)

Aids Director in planning and directing some or all aspects of library or library system. May manage a major aspect of the library operation (e.g., technical services, public services, collection development, systems/automation).

University

	MEAN	FIRST QUARTILE	MEDIAN	THIRD QUARTILE
North Atlantic N=104 Range=$23,500-$122,390	61,852	47,183	59,495	76,723
Great Lakes & Plains N=61 Range=$20,500-$80,000	53,111	41,539	53,421	65,000
Southeast N=81 Range=$25,000-$94,200	52,669	42,700	52,227	63,200
West & Southwest N=56 Range=$33,508-$81,700	57,467	47,803	56,049	68,231
All Regions N=302 Range=$20,500-$122,390	56,810	44,982	55,533	66,680

All Academic and Public Libraries

	MEAN	FIRST QUARTILE	MEDIAN	THIRD QUARTILE
North Atlantic N=277 Range=$23,500-$126,980	57,976	45,500	55,680	68,855
Great Lakes & Plains N=173 Range=$20,500-$102,792	48,938	36,000	46,137	62,580
Southeast N=222 Range=$23,000-$94,200	48,383	38,874	47,594	57,036
West & Southwest N=203 Range=$23,000-$104,588	53,211	41,511	52,272	63,120
All Regions N=875 Range=$20,500-$126,980	52,650	40,057	51,057	63,658

SOURCE: ALA SURVEY OF LIBRARIAN SALARIES, 1996

Department Head/Branch Head
(Page 1 of 3)

Manages operation of a library unit that is physically separate from the main library (e.g., a branch or a department library) or of one aspect of the main library (e.g., Reference Department, Serials Department, Children's Department).

Medium-sized Public Library
(Serving a population of from 25,000 to 99,999)

	MEAN	FIRST QUARTILE	MEDIAN	THIRD QUARTILE
North Atlantic N=197 Range=$22,000-$69,970	41,134	32,367	40,322	47,705
Great Lakes & Plains N=174 Range=$19,419-$54,938	36,808	32,057	36,773	41,675
Southeast N=68 Range=$19,573-$52,981	31,945	25,454	30,267	35,960
West & Southwest N=72 Range=$20,244-$53,019	38,494	30,500	39,813	46,356
All Regions N=511 Range=$19,419-$69,970	38,066	30,862	37,044	43,355

Large Public Library
(Serving a population of 100,000 or more)

	MEAN	FIRST QUARTILE	MEDIAN	THIRD QUARTILE
North Atlantic N=446 Range=$20,291-$72,164	43,497	38,052	42,760	47,804
Great Lakes & Plains N=422 Range=$18,482-$66,924	44,459	38,854	43,743	49,940
Southeast N=425 Range=$20,193-$65,040	39,738	32,968	39,354	46,176
West & Southwest N=471 Range=$21,840-$67,954	44,373	36,360	43,791	52,718
All Regions N=1,764 Range=$18,482-$72,164	43,056	36,681	42,507	48,826

SOURCE: ALA SURVEY OF LIBRARIAN SALARIES, 1996

Department Head/Branch Head (Page 2 of 3)

Manages operation of a library unit that is physically separate from the main library (e.g., a branch or a department library) or of one aspect of the main library (e.g., Reference Department, Serials Department, Children's Department).

Two-Year College

	MEAN	FIRST QUARTILE	MEDIAN	THIRD QUARTILE
North Atlantic N=17 Range=$31,764-$74,667	50,993	43,000	45,737	62,003
Great Lakes & Plains N=12 Range=$35,060-$55,200	42,066	39,640	40,786	41,573
Southeast N=10 Range=$30,408-$45,103	38,702	35,538	38,373	42,641
West & Southwest N=20 Range=$28,188-$61,363	42,539	36,900	42,854	46,944
All Regions N=59 Range=$28,188-$74,667	44,228	37,889	41,796	48,000

Four-Year College

	MEAN	FIRST QUARTILE	MEDIAN	THIRD QUARTILE
North Atlantic N=24 Range=$23,376-$62,000	40,672	28,927	39,958	49,810
Great Lakes & Plains N=13 Range=$26,000-$51,989	37,560	34,127	36,448	40,800
Southeast N=23 Range=$18,000-$41,091	31,857	24,000	32,690	38,000
West & Southwest N=10 Range=$23,000-$59,976	35,908	29,943	34,890	36,024
All Regions N=70 Range=$18,000-$62,000	36,517	29,355	35,737	40,915

SOURCE: ALA SURVEY OF LIBRARIAN SALARIES, 1996

Department Head/Branch Head (Page 3 of 3)

Manages operation of a library unit that is physically separate from the main library (e.g., a branch or a department library) or of one aspect of the main library (e.g., Reference Department, Serials Department, Children's Department).

University

	MEAN	FIRST QUARTILE	MEDIAN	THIRD QUARTILE
North Atlantic N=316 Range=$25,000-$93,100	48,609	39,752	47,007	55,696
Great Lakes & Plains N=233 Range=$27,290-$78,052	43,893	37,410	41,901	50,004
Southeast N=225 Range=$24,600-$76,100	41,703	35,111	40,539	47,400
West & Southwest N=191 Range=$25,750-$71,196	44,712	38,300	43,452	51,791
All Regions N=965 Range=$24,600-$93,100	45,089	37,565	43,530	51,561

All Academic and Public Libraries

	MEAN	FIRST QUARTILE	MEDIAN	THIRD QUARTILE
North Atlantic N=1000 Range=$20,291-$93,100	44,707	37,307	43,369	50,318
Great Lakes & Plains N=854 Range=$18,482-$78,052	42,607	36,075	41,932	48,413
Southeast N=751 Range=$18,000-$76,100	39,366	32,218	38,805	45,531
West & Southwest N=764 Range=$20,244-$71,196	43,745	36,241	43,099	51,196
All Regions N=3369 Range=$18,000-$93,100	42,766	35,693	41,914	48,774

SOURCE: ALA SURVEY OF LIBRARIAN SALARIES, 1996

Reference/Information Librarian
(Page 1 of 3)

Locates information for library users or helps users find it in print or electronic sources. Answers questions and gives instruction about the use of sources in the library or available electronically. Makes decisions about acquiring or arranging for access to them.

Medium-sized Public Library
(Serving a population of from 25,000 to 99,999)

	MEAN	FIRST QUARTILE	MEDIAN	THIRD QUARTILE
North Atlantic N=187 Range=$21,840-$64,264	36,906	31,072	36,000	41,369
Great Lakes & Plains N=160 Range=$20,280-$43,680	30,959	27,045	30,480	34,341
Southeast N=34 Range=$19,961-$42,436	28,492	24,500	26,406	31,108
West & Southwest N=71 Range=$21,744-$49,344	34,497	28,785	33,530	39,663
All Regions N=452 Range=$19,961-$64,264	33,789	28,585	32,803	38,507

Large Public Library
(Serving a population of 100,000 or more)

	MEAN	FIRST QUARTILE	MEDIAN	THIRD QUARTILE
North Atlantic N=450 Range=$18,700-$52,155	35,079	29,812	35,033	39,274
Great Lakes & Plains N=465 Range=$19,676-$60,648	36,005	32,594	35,339	39,668
Southeast N=398 Range=$20,000-$60,392	32,436	26,728	31,555	37,207
West & Southwest N=479 Range=$21,996-$58,872	37,047	31,283	36,254	42,994
All Regions N=1,792 Range=$18,700-$60,648	35,258	29,952	34,528	39,668

SOURCE: ALA SURVEY OF LIBRARIAN SALARIES, 1996

Reference/Information Librarian (Page 2 of 3)

Locates information for library users or helps users find it in print or electronic sources. Answers questions and gives instruction about the use of sources in the library or available electronically. Makes decisions about acquiring sources or arranging for access to them.

Two-Year College

	MEAN	FIRST QUARTILE	MEDIAN	THIRD QUARTILE
North Atlantic N=58 Range=$23,977-$77,964	42,252	33,310	41,178	46,093
Great Lakes & Plains N=23 Range=$24,000-$74,825	51,700	35,173	45,930	71,283
Southeast N=31 Range=$26,500-$60,065	35,858	29,357	32,460	40,000
West & Southwest N=38 Range=$25,000-$83,461	42,699	32,105	41,684	49,000
All Regions N=150 Range=$23,977-$83,461	42,493	32,000	40,216	48,480

Four-Year College

	MEAN	FIRST QUARTILE	MEDIAN	THIRD QUARTILE
North Atlantic N=44 Range=$20,900-$61,134	34,844	27,338	34,521	40,200
Great Lakes & Plains N=34 Range=$23,000-$60,815	33,260	28,500	30,173	34,765
Southeast N=24 Range=$20,000-$51,417	29,924	24,733	28,639	32,902
West & Southwest N=18 Range=$21,000-$88,080	38,579	28,321	33,420	40,524
All Regions N=120 Range=$20,000-$88,080	33,971	27,603	30,856	37,182

SOURCE: ALA SURVEY OF LIBRARIAN SALARIES, 1996

Reference/Information Librarian (Page 3 of 3)

Locates information for library users or helps users find it in print or electronic sources. Answers questions and gives instruction about the use of sources in the library or available electronically. Makes decisions about acquiring sources or arranging for access to them.

University

	MEAN	FIRST QUARTILE	MEDIAN	THIRD QUARTILE
North Atlantic N=273 Range=$21,600-$69,870	38,993	32,342	37,594	44,106
Great Lakes & Plains N=238 Range=$18,000-$86,184	36,937	29,844	33,572	41,064
Southeast N=212 Range=$21,000-$66,826	34,282	29,311	33,092	39,019
West & Southwest N=233 Range=$21,025-$89,237	36,818	29,750	35,589	40,863
All Regions N=956 Range=$18,000-$89,237	36,906	30,068	34,866	41,269

All Academic and Public Libraries

	MEAN	FIRST QUARTILE	MEDIAN	THIRD QUARTILE
North Atlantic N=1,012 Range=$18,700-$77,964	36,873	30,968	36,009	41,132
Great Lakes & Plains N=920 Range=$18,000-$86,184	35,660	30,202	33,990	39,350
Southeast N=699 Range=$19,961-$66,826	32,869	27,248	31,900	37,143
West & Southwest N=839 Range=$21,000-$89,237	37,056	30,663	35,760	42,444
All Regions N=3,470 Range=$18,000-$89,237	35,789	29,812	34,409	39,996

SOURCE: ALA SURVEY OF LIBRARIAN SALARIES, 1996

Cataloger and/or Classifier
(Page 1 of 3)

Organizes all types of material purchased by the library. Describes each item in standard format and assigns access points. Assigns subject headings and classification numbers. Uses automated systems. May be involved with only descriptive cataloging or only subject cataloging/classification.

Medium-sized Public Library
(Serving a population of from 25,000 to 99,999)

	MEAN	FIRST QUARTILE	MEDIAN	THIRD QUARTILE
North Atlantic N=36 Range=$24,217-$53,093	36,271	30,833	36,026	40,723
Great Lakes & Plains N=44 Range=$18,243-$41,945	30,630	26,000	30,560	34,828
Southeast N=19 Range=$20,000-$40,000	28,476	24,960	26,988	33,490
West & Southwest N=21 Range=$17,800-$48,370	32,589	26,810	32,006	40,104
All Regions N=120 Range=$17,800-$53,093	32,324	26,328	31,493	38,091

Large Public Library
(Serving a population of 100,000 or more)

	MEAN	FIRST QUARTILE	MEDIAN	THIRD QUARTILE
North Atlantic N=62 Range=$22,500-$56,589	36,257	30,090	35,473	42,238
Great Lakes & Plains N=60 Range=$24,761-$60,904	36,409	32,081	35,481	39,568
Southeast N=68 Range=$23,171-$51,613	34,917	29,342	33,186	40,890
West & Southwest N=65 Range=$21,996-$53,140	37,403	31,296	35,859	42,994
All Regions N=255 Range=$21,996-$60,904	36,228	30,563	35,217	41,477

SOURCE: ALA SURVEY OF LIBRARIAN SALARIES, 1996

Cataloger and/or Classifier (Page 2 of 3)

Organizes all types of material purchased by the library. Describes each item in standard format and assigns access points. Assigns subject headings and classification numbers. Uses automated systems. May be involved with only descriptive cataloging or only subject cataloging/classification.

Two-Year College

	MEAN	FIRST QUARTILE	MEDIAN	THIRD QUARTILE
North Atlantic N=17 Range=$23,533-$74,000	45,594	35,948	40,851	57,302
Great Lakes & Plains N=14 Range=$25,000-$86,667	52,217	40,000	51,104	67,724
Southeast N=9 Range=$28,032-$61,589	39,777	32,112	36,600	46,489
West & Southwest N=16 Range=$27,000-$57,903	40,176	32,050	40,148	45,604
All Regions N=56 Range=$23,533-$86,667	44,767	33,182	40,843	52,911

Four-Year College

	MEAN	FIRST QUARTILE	MEDIAN	THIRD QUARTILE
North Atlantic N=18 Range=$26,000-$64,600	36,011	30,339	34,641	39,120
Great Lakes & Plains N=14 Range=$20,000-$49,592	31,140	26,000	28,959	36,733
Southeast N=16 Range=$19,000-$39,228	28,726	25,887	28,273	32,169
West & Southwest N=9 Range=$24,360-$55,560	35,923	28,400	36,037	39,090
All Regions N=57 Range=$19,000-$64,600	32,756	26,800	30,684	37,464

SOURCE: ALA SURVEY OF LIBRARIAN SALARIES, 1996

Cataloger and/or Classifier (Page 3 of 3)

Organizes all types of material purchased by the library. Describes each item in standard format and assigns access points. Assigns subject headings and classification numbers. Uses automated systems. May be involved with only descriptive cataloging or only subject cataloging/classification.

University

	MEAN	FIRST QUARTILE	MEDIAN	THIRD QUARTILE
North Atlantic N=174 Range=$24,048-$62,092	40,380	35,580	39,344	45,093
Great Lakes & Plains N=91 Range=$23,144-$62,128	35,698	30,105	33,404	41,187
Southeast N=109 Range=$21,000-$48,600	34,018	29,591	32,656	38,160
West & Southwest N=91 Range=$20,000-$83,129	37,584	30,672	36,000	42,000
All Regions N=465 Range=$20,000-$83,129	37,425	31,825	36,123	42,200

All Academic and Public Libraries

	MEAN	FIRST QUARTILE	MEDIAN	THIRD QUARTILE
North Atlantic N=307 Range=$22,500-$74,000	39,098	33,333	38,136	43,781
Great Lakes & Plains N=223 Range=$18,243-$86,667	35,640	29,852	33,676	39,668
Southeast N=221 Range=$19,000-$61,589	33,669	28,900	32,264	38,915
West & Southwest N=202 Range=$17,800-$83,129	37,138	30,672	35,930	42,073
All Regions N=953 Range=$17,800-$86,667	36,614	30,318	35,500	41,392

SOURCE: ALA SURVEY OF LIBRARIAN SALARIES, 1996

Children's and/or Young Adult Services Librarian
(Page 1 of 2)

Plans and conducts library services for children and/or young adults. Advises on reading materials. Selects materials for the collection. May plan and conduct special programs and outreach services.

Medium-sized Public Library
(Serving a population of from 25,000 to 99,999)

	MEAN	FIRST QUARTILE	MEDIAN	THIRD QUARTILE
North Atlantic N=94 Range=$23,322-$63,475	36,755	31,599	34,526	39,786
Great Lakes & Plains N=66 Range=$18,187-$49,122	30,309	26,490	30,181	33,545
Southeast N=21 Range=$21,341-$42,192	27,498	23,784	25,492	29,119
West & Southwest N=37 Range=$20,800-$49,344	34,558	28,176	33,259	40,339
All Regions N=218 Range=$18,187-$63,475	33,539	28,080	32,375	37,807

Large Public Library
(Serving a population of 100,000 or more)

	MEAN	FIRST QUARTILE	MEDIAN	THIRD QUARTILE
North Atlantic N=200 Range=$23,623-$58,774	35,845	31,353	35,284	39,828
Great Lakes & Plains N=211 Range=$21,195-$60,648	34,782	29,852	33,607	39,528
Southeast N=120 Range=$20,875-$48,152	31,065	25,644	29,266	35,451
West & Southwest N=246 Range=$21,996-$51,210	35,981	30,467	35,760	38,754
All Regions N=777 Range=$20,875-$60,648	34,861	29,614	33,990	38,805

SOURCE: ALA SURVEY OF LIBRARIAN SALARIES, 1996

Children's and/or Young Adult Services Librarian (Page 2 of 2)

Plans and conducts library services for children and/or young adults. Advises on reading materials. Selects materials for the collection. May plan and conduct special programs and outreach services.

All Public Libraries

	MEAN	FIRST QUARTILE	MEDIAN	THIRD QUARTILE
North Atlantic N=294 Range=$23,322-$63,475	36,136	31,522	35,033	39,786
Great Lakes & Plains N=277 Range=$18,187-$60,648	33,716	29,023	33,184	37,608
Southeast N=141 Range=$20,875-$48,152	30,534	25,000	28,932	35,235
West & Southwest N=283 Range=$20,800-$51,210	35,795	30,096	35,669	39,732
All Regions N=995 Range=$18,187-$63,475	34,572	29,023	33,751	38,754

SOURCE: ALA SURVEY OF LIBRARIAN SALARIES, 1996

Beginning Librarian

Full-time staff member with a master's degree from a program in library and information studies accredited by ALA, but no professional experience.

Medium-sized Public Library
(Serving a population of from 25,000 to 99,999)

	MEAN	FIRST QUARTILE	MEDIAN	THIRD QUARTILE
North Atlantic N=22 Range=$21,000-$33,800	28,171	25,823	28,950	30,000
Great Lakes & Plains N=17 Range=$19,000-$31,000	24,617	22,500	24,620	27,040
Southeast N=6 Range=$18,278-$38,000	24,700	21,500	22,769	24,884
West & Southwest N=7 Range=$21,000-$34,020	25,771	21,744	24,162	30,168
All Regions N=52 Range=$18,278-$38,000	26,285	22,611	26,008	29,869

Large Public Library
(Serving a population of 100,000 or more)

	MEAN	FIRST QUARTILE	MEDIAN	THIRD QUARTILE
North Atlantic N=34 Range=$25,649-$33,728	27,420	26,152	27,138	27,985
Great Lakes & Plains N=49 Range=$19,573-$32,487	27,293	26,620	26,911	28,205
Southeast N=60 Range=$20,000-$31,799	25,753	23,999	24,949	28,140
West & Southwest N=83 Range=$20,940-$43,274	31,272	24,720	27,040	43,274
All Regions N=226 Range=$19,573-$43,274	28,365	25,131	26,805	28,750

SOURCE: ALA SURVEY OF LIBRARIAN SALARIES, 1996

Beginning Librarian (Page 2 of 3)

Full-time staff member with a master's degree from a program in library and information studies accredited by ALA, but no professional experience.

Two-Year College

	MEAN	FIRST QUARTILE	MEDIAN	THIRD QUARTILE
North Atlantic N=6 Range=$26,000-$39,140	31,408	27,600	29,417	36,875
Great Lakes & Plains N=4 Range=$24,000-$42,667	32,492	27,171	31,650	37,812
Southeast N=3 Range=$27,500-$29,333	28,611	27,500	29,000	29,333
West & Southwest N=13 Range=$23,000-$37,200	31,044	30,000	31,708	33,080
All Regions N=26 Range=$23,000-$42,667	31,070	28,188	30,568	33,080

Four-Year College

	MEAN	FIRST QUARTILE	MEDIAN	THIRD QUARTILE
North Atlantic N=10 Range=$24,000-$44,667	32,130	27,500	31,600	35,000
Great Lakes & Plains N=1 Range=$26,500-$26,500	26,500	26,500	26,500	26,500
Southeast N=5 Range=$19,000-$30,000	24,200	21,000	25,000	26,000
West & Southwest N=4 Range=$26,040-$32,000	28,020	26,040	27,020	30,000
All Regions N=20 Range=$19,000-$44,667	29,044	25,500	27,750	32,000

SOURCE: ALA SURVEY OF LIBRARIAN SALARIES, 1996

Beginning Librarian (Page 3 of 3)

Full-time staff member with a master's degree from a program in library and information studies accredited by ALA, but no professional experience.

University

	MEAN	FIRST QUARTILE	MEDIAN	THIRD QUARTILE
North Atlantic N=25 Range=$23,920-$49,920	34,934	28,000	33,400	41,200
Great Lakes & Plains N=28 Range=$20,500-$32,196	27,090	25,000	27,000	28,500
Southeast N=27 Range=$21,000-$39,100	28,324	25,000	28,000	30,000
West & Southwest N=29 Range=$23,000-$45,756	29,710	25,000	27,000	30,000
All Regions N=109 Range=$20,500-$49,920	29,892	26,000	28,000	32,011

All Academic and Public Libraries

	MEAN	FIRST QUARTILE	MEDIAN	THIRD QUARTILE
North Atlantic N=97 Range=$21,000-$49,920	30,259	26,500	28,162	32,300
Great Lakes & Plains N=99 Range=$19,000-$42,667	26,978	25,971	26,911	28,205
Southeast N=101 Range=$18,278-$39,100	26,386	24,500	25,865	28,900
West & Southwest N=136 Range=$20,940-$45,756	30,538	25,000	27,498	34,691
All Regions N=433 Range=$18,278-$49,920	28,693	25,000	27,040	30,000

SOURCE: ALA SURVEY OF LIBRARIAN SALARIES, 1996

Discussion

Summary of Results

People interested in a particular type of library or a particular type of work, or a particular region will have their own way of drawing conclusions from the results of this survey. However, the results may be summarized in a very general way by observing mean salaries paid to particular positions, mean salaries paid by particular types of libraries, or mean salaries paid in particular parts of the U.S.

Salaries by Position

The six positions are shown in rank order by mean of salaries paid on Table 1. Two additional columns are also given: a column showing the dollar amount of change from 1995 to 1996 and a column indicating the percent of increase.

Table 1. Rank Order of Position Titles by Mean of Salaries Paid

Title	96 Salary	95 Salary	Change Amount	%
Director	58,297	58,220	+ 77	+ .13
Deputy/Associate/Assistant Director	52,650	51,242	+1,408	+2.74
Department Head/Branch Head	42,766	42,176	+ 590	+1.39
Reference/Information Librarian	35,789	35,649	+140	+ .39
Cataloger and/or Classifier	36,614	36,274	+340	+ .93
Children's and/or Young Adult Services Librarian	34,572	35,006	-434	-1.23

SOURCE: ALA SURVEY OF LIBRARIAN SALARIES, 1996

The average of the percent of increase over the past year is less than one percent (.725%). The figure is much lower than the increase in comparable occupations reported by the U.S. Bureau of Labor Statistics (BLS) in the June 1996 *Monthly Labor Review*. A table entitled "Employment Cost Index, wages and salaries by occupation and industry group" shows that civilian workers consisting of "private industry workers, (excluding farm and household workers) and state and local government (excluding federal government) workers" received an average 3.2 percent increase for the twelve months ending in March 1996. White collar workers received an average increase of 3.4 percent for the same time period.

Table 2 shows the percent change in mean salaries for the six positions in each of the last seven years. Commenting on the first five of those years in the 1993 report we noted that librarian salaries were increasing at a decreasing rate. That trend changed in the 1994 report and the 1995 increases were higher again. The trend reversed sharply in 1996.

Table 2. Percent Change in Mean of Salaries Paid 1988-1996

Title	88 to 89 %	89 to 90 %	90 to 91 %	91 to 92 %	92 to 93 %	93 to 94 %	94 to 95 %	95 to 96 %
Director	+9	+2.0	+8.9	+6.0	+3.9	+4.4	+4.5	+.13
Deputy/Associate/Assistant Director	+14	+3.5	+8.9	+4.0	+0.2	+3.4	+5.3	+2.7
Department Head/Branch Head	+12	+4.5	+7.8	+5.7	+0.9	+3.0	+4.0	+1.3
Reference/Information Librarian	+9	+6.2	+5.1	+3.2	+1.5	+3.7	+4.1	+.39
Cataloger and/or Classifier	+13	+5.9	+5.2	+2.8	-0.5	+4.1	+6.9	+.93
Children's and/or Young Adult Services Librarian	+15	+6.4	+8.0	+11.3	-2.1	+3.3	+4.2	-1.2

SOURCE: ALA SURVEY OF LIBRARIAN SALARIES, 1996

Salaries by Type of Library

When one considers salaries by type of library, it is useful to separate positions into three groups: the administrative positions found in all types of libraries (Director, Deputy/Associate/Assistant Director, Department Head/Branch Head); the other two positions found in all libraries (Reference/Information Librarian, Cataloger and/or Classifier); and the one position found only in public libraries (Children's and/or Young Adult Services Librarian).

The mean of salaries paid is highest in large public libraries for Director and for Deputy/Associate/Assistant Director and highest in university libraries for Department Head/Branch Head The mean is lowest in four-year colleges for all three administrative positions. For the other two common positions, the mean is always highest in two-year colleges and lowest in medium-sized public libraries. For the position found only in public libraries--Children's and/or Young Adult Services Librarian--the mean of salaries paid is higher in large public libraries.

Salaries by Region of the U.S.

In order to determine which region has the highest salaries, we analyzed the six positions and the five library size/type categories. When the region with the highest mean salary was marked for each position in each size/type category, North Atlantic was checked 70 percent of the time, West and Southwest was checked 15 percent of the time as was, Great Lakes and Plains. Southeast was never highest. This pattern is similar to last year except that the percent for North Atlantic is 10 points higher and the percent for West and Southwest is 14 point lower. The lowest mean salary was in the Southeast over 92 percent of the time. This pattern is similar to what has been observed in all previous surveys in this series.

Complicating Factors

When designing this survey over twelve years ago, we were aware that several aspects of the patterns of employment in libraries would complicate our efforts. As we talked with respondents and users of the reports over the years, we gained additional insights into several factors which should be taken into consideration when using these results.

The Meaning of "Full-Time"

The questionnaire asked about salaries for **full-time** positions only, but full-time was not defined. There are at least two problems in this area: How many months in a year is full-time? How do you report people who work full-time in the library but part-time at one job and part-time at another?

The months in a year problem primarily affects academic libraries where librarians sometimes have academic year contracts for less than twelve months. In this survey, respondents are asked to indicate the number of months a salary covers and the computer calculated twelve months at the same rate. Appendix G shows how often less-than-twelve-month salaries occur.

Another complication related to the issue of "full-time" is the fact that one librarian may fill more than one position. For example: a public librarian may work part-time as a children's librarian and part-time as a cataloger; an academic librarian may be a reference librarian as well as a department head (of reference department). Survey instructions told the respondent:

> If a staff member works full-time but performs duties of more than one position, list him or her as incumbent in the position which you consider his or her major responsibility. **List each staff member only once.**

The Meaning of "Professional"

In the early years of this survey, respondents were asked to report only salaries paid to professionals, but the word "professional" was not defined. Instead, each position was described in such a way that professional responsibility was clearly implied. Instructions told the respondent to list all incumbents in these positions "regardless of academic credentials." We accepted the judgment of the respondent that the salaries reported were for professional work but found out, when we called about low salaries (see below), that some respondents had doubts about whether a particular incumbent could be described as "professional." When such doubts were expressed, we asked the respondent to make a decision based on the definition in ALA's statement on "Library Education and Personnel Utilization." (See Appendix B, Policy 54.1, Section 8.) In 1990, that definition was added to the instructions.

Beginning with the 1991 survey, we asked respondents to report only staff *with master's degrees from programs in library and information studies accredited by ALA*. The questionnaire requested information which helped to ensure that only salaries for professional positions were included in this report. Following each position title and description was a line for "Position Title (if different from above)." When screening revealed such titles as "secretary," "library assistant" or "technical assistant" on that line, the salary information was not used.

Salaries Below $20,000

In previous years this report has described the methodology used to determine the cut-off point below which salaries were dropped as probably not being for full-time, professional work. The cut-off point for the 1996 survey was $20,000. Of the 11,046 salaries initially entered into the file, fifty were below $20,000 (less than 1%). Staff at the Library Research Center conducted telephone interviews with directors at the twenty seven libraries involved and learned that thirty were for part-time work, non-professional positions, or were paid to staff without the specified degree. Those thirty salaries were dropped from the file used for the report. Once the thirty salaries were dropped, the total was 11,016 salaries. The dropped salaries had been reported primarily because the respondent had misunderstood the instructions. Twenty salaries of less than $20,000 did remain in the file. Sixteen were in public libraries and four were in academic libraries.

Job Levels or Faculty Ranks

The wording of this questionnaire is based on an assumption that librarians are compensated at a particular amount for doing a particular job (e.g., reference). However, in many libraries that is not true. Some libraries use a system of levels in their compensation structure (e.g., Librarian I, II, III, IV) to account for the background a person brings to a job and the amount of responsibility it entails. Compensation is based on level, not on the type of work done as defined by our position descriptions. Some academic libraries pay salaries based on faculty rank rather than work done. In many academic libraries where librarians have faculty rank and titles, they are compensated as Instructor, Assistant Professor, Associate Professor or Professor and not as any one of the position titles on our questionnaire. We do not attempt to account for this variety within the structure of our questionnaire and every year some respondents tell us it was impossible to complete the questionnaire for this reason.

Several respondents and reviewers of this report have recommended in the past that we collect salary data for librarian levels or ranks. We have considered this seriously, but concluded that it would be at least as confusing as the current method due to the fact that levels and ranks mean different things in different libraries.

Longevity Pay

Some large public libraries were unable to report exact salaries for each position due to the large number of incumbents and the small amount of time available. In several such cases, respondents reported the number of incumbents for a position that were in a specific range on the salary schedule and we used the midpoint of that range for the appropriate number of incumbents. While reasonable in a national study that reports summary statistics, this procedure does not take into account longevity pay which is related to individual tenure and not to a point on the salary schedule. Thus some incumbents may be earning more than is reported here.

Level of Experience

Respondents occasionally ask us to ask for and report salaries in a way that takes into account the years of experience that an incumbent possesses. Unfortunately, providing that information would be a burden on respondents and reporting it would make this report overly complex. This report does take such factors into account in two ways: beginning librarian salaries are reported in a separate table and are not included in salary data for specific positions; and data for specific positions show figures at the first and third quartile as well as the mean, median, and range.

Appendix A

Compensation Surveys Providing Information on Library Workers

Most library salary surveys listed below are conducted on a regular schedule (annual or biennial) and on a regional or national basis. Several surveys that were in earlier editions of this publication have been dropped in this listing because the latest surveys contained data collected prior to 1994. These include surveys by the ACRL New England Chapter, American Bar Association, Art Libraries Society of North America, and *Library Mosaics* (support staff). If new surveys are conducted by these groups in the future, they will be included in the next annual listing.

The library literature should be monitored for reports of one-time surveys by individual libraries or associations. Some state library agencies collect salary and benefits data as part of their ongoing statistical gathering efforts from libraries within their own state. There is wide variation, however, in what data are collected and how these are compiled and reported. Most collect only public library data. Academic and school library data may be collected by other state agencies.

In addition, some state library associations collect salary data, issue recommended salary guidelines, set minimum salaries for professional positions, or publish reports in association journals or newsletters. As of June 1996, nineteen states had established recommended minimum salaries. These include: Connecticut, Delaware, Illinois, Indiana, Iowa, Louisiana, Maine, Massachusetts, New Jersey, North Carolina, Ohio, Pennsylvania, Rhode Island, South Carolina, South Dakota, Texas, Vermont, West Virginia, and Wisconsin. Specific amounts are not listed here because these are regularly updated by the associations. The latest figures can be found in the most recent classified section of *American Libraries* or *College & Research Libraries News*. A list of state library agency and association addresses can be found in *The Bowker Annual: Library and Book Trade Almanac*.

Individual libraries will sometimes conduct private surveys of institutions of comparable size or in the same geographical area, either through an outside consulting firm or by calling libraries informally. For the most part, these surveys are not published, although the initiating library will often share results with participating libraries. Some library workers are also conducting surveys that compare their salaries with other professions and occupations within their jurisdiction in an effort to achieve pay equity with positions requiring comparable skills, effort, responsibilities and working conditions.

Academic Libraries

Association of Research Libraries. *ARL Annual Salary Survey*. Washington, D.C.: ARL, 1973-.

The annual survey shows the number of filled positions, average years of experience, and average, median and beginning salaries for professional positions in all ARL libraries. In addition, tables present the number of staff, average salaries, and years of experience for position categories and display findings on the present incumbents of these positions by sex and minority group membership, and by geographical location, size, and type of institution. Salaries for staff in law and medical libraries are presented in two separate series of tables. Salary data for staff in Canadian university libraries are also displayed in Canadian dollars.

Order from ARL, 21 DuPont Circle, NW, Washington, D.C. 20036, 202/296-2296, fax 202/872-0884. The 1995-96 survey is available for $35/ARL members or $65/nonmembers, plus $5 s/h per publication.

College and University Personnel Association. *1995-96 Administrative Compensation Survey*. Washington, D.C.: CUPA.

Annual survey; 1995-96 survey includes data on 170 college and university administrative positions from 1,384 public and private institutions. The tables in the survey present the median salary and salary percentiles according to institutional budget, enrollment, and classification. Directors of library services are included, as well as catalog, acquisitions, reference, technical and public services librarians.

The survey is available from CUPA, 1233 20th St., NW, Suite 301, Washington, D.C. 20035-1250, 202/429-0311; $80 for association members, $180 for non-members/survey participants and $300 for non-members/survey non-participants.

Public Libraries

American Library Association. Public Library Association. *Public Library Data Service Statistical Report*. Chicago: PLA.

Annual listing with information that includes library-specific salaries for directors and beginning librarians for most public libraries serving 100,000 or more and for many smaller libraries, as well as basic library statistics. The 1996 edition is available from ALA Customer Services Dept., 155 N. Wacker Dr., Chicago, IL 60606-1719, 800/545-2433, press 7, for $75 with the usual discounts for PLA and ALA members.

Gwen Hall. "Salaries of Municipal Officials, 1995" in *The Municipal Year Book* 1996. Washington, D.C.: International City/County Management Association.

Chief librarian salaries for local public libraries are included with earnings of other city department heads.

These are reported by geographic region, population size, city type (i.e., central, suburban, independent) and form of government. The mean, median, and first and third quartiles are included for libraries serving ten different population groups ranging from under 2,500 to over 1,000,000. *The Municipal Year Book* is published in April of each year and includes salary data for previous year. For details, contact Gwen Hall, ICMA, 777 N. Capitol St., Suite 500, Washington, D.C. 20002, 202/962-3651.

Sandstedt, Carl R. *Salary Survey: West-North-Central States.* St. Peters, Mo.: St. Charles City-County Library.

Annual survey provides data for directors, assistant directors, department heads, starting MLS, and several support positions for public libraries in West-North-Central States (North Dakota, South Dakota, Nebraska, Kansas, Minnesota, Iowa, Missouri). Average salaries are presented by size of library budget. Also includes per FTE costs, per capita support, per capita materials budget.

Usually available in April for current calendar year. Send $5.00 for first copy, $2.00 per additional copy. Diskettes with spreadsheet files are $10. Please prepay. A $5 invoicing fee will be made for all orders requiring an invoice. Contact "Salary Survey," St. Charles City-County Library, 425 Spencer Rd., Box 529, St. Peters, MO 63376, 314/441-2300.

School Libraries

Educational Research Service. *National Survey of Salaries and Wages in Public Schools.* Arlington, Va.: ERS.

Since 1974-75, ERS has published an annual report of salaries for public school personnel, which includes data for school librarians and library clerks. Usually published in three volumes, the report covers scheduled salaries for professional personnel and actual salaries paid for professional and support personnel by enrollment group, per pupil expenditure, and geographic region.

The 1995-96 report costs $60 for each of the three volumes, updated annually. Available from ERS, 2000 Clarendon Blvd., Arlington, VA 22201, 703/243-2100.

Miller, Marilyn L., and Schontz, Marilyn. "Expenditures for Resources in School Library Media Centers," *School Library Journal.*

As part of a report every two years on budgets for and expenditures by school library media centers, some median and mean salary data for media specialists are reported by level of school. Included are comparisons of schools with and without district level library media coordinators. October 1995 issue has the latest data.

National Education Association. *Estimates of School Statistics*. Washington, D.C.: NEA.

Annual statistical data for the 50 states and District of Columbia includes estimated average annual salaries of total instructional staff and also separate data for classroom teachers by state and region. Librarian data are not given separately, however, but are grouped with teachers, principals, supervisors, guidance and psychological personnel and related instructional workers.

The 1995-96 annual report is available beginning late summer, 1996. Contact NEA Professional Library, PO Box 509, West Haven, CT 06516, 203/934-2669, 800-229-4200.

Specialized Libraries

American Association of Law Libraries. *Biennial Salary Survey 1995*. Chicago: AALL, 1995.

The report summarizes salary information for all library types, with three following sections that cover academic libraries, private firm/corporate libraries and state, court and county libraries. The data is broken out by nine geographical regions in the U.S., and further broken down for most large cities within those regions.

The price for the publication is $60 for AALL members, $100 for non-members (includes shipping). Contact Steven Serpas, Publications Assistant, AALL, 53 W. Jackson Blvd., Suite 940, Chicago, IL 60604, 312/939-4764, fax 312/431-1097.

Association of Academic Health Sciences Library Directors. *Annual Statistics of Medical School Libraries in the United States and Canada*. Seattle, Washington.

Salaries are provided for director, associate director, division head, department head, other librarians, and entry level positions. Minimum, maximum and mean are provided for the positions and arranged by region.

Salary data for 1994-95 are included in the 18th edition. It is available at a cost of $50 for members of the Association of Academic Health Sciences Library Directors and $100 for nonmembers. This edition and previous editions may be ordered by contacting AAHSLD, 2033 Sixth Ave., #804, Seattle, WA 98121, 206/441-6020. The 1995-96 edition will be available following Spring of 1997.

Medical Library Association. *Health Sciences Librarian Compensation: Results of MLA's 1995 Salary Survey*. Chicago: MLA.

Triennial survey data cover geographic area, position level, type of institution, years of experience, education, primary area of responsibility, benefits, and other information.

The 1995 MLA member salary survey is available at a cost of $35.00 for members; $60.00 for non-members from MLA, 6 N. Michigan Ave., Suite 300, Chicago, IL 60602, 312/419-9094.

Special Libraries Association. *SLA Biennial Salary Survey*. Washington, D.C.: SLA.

Since 1967, SLA conducted an in-depth salary survey of members every three years. As of 1990, the in-depth survey is conducted every two years. Results are now issued as separate publications. Salaries are reported at the 25th, 50th (median) and 75th percentiles and contain breakdowns by industry, geographic region, administrative responsibility, sex, education level, and experience. Data for the U.S. and Canada are presented in separate tables. Annual updates, using a random sampling of 25 percent of the membership and an abbreviated questionnaire, were started in 1977 and are used in years between the now biennial surveys. The results of the updates are published in *Special Libraries* in the fall issue.

The 1995 update appeared in the fall 1995 issue of *Special Libraries*. Data collected in 1996 will be published in October. The report will sell for $36 (members); $45 (non-members). Contact Special Libraries Association, 1700 18th St., N.W., Washington, D.C. 20009, 202/234-4700.

Other

Association for Library and Information Science Education. *Library and Information Science Education Statistical Report*. Ann Arbor, MI.: ALISE, 1980-.

Average and median salaries for faculty and administrators in ALISE member schools are provided in this annual report by sex, rank and term of appointment.

Back issues (1981-) of the report are available from ALISE, c/o University of Michigan, School of Information, 550 E. University, 304 West Bldg., Ann Arbor, MI 48109-1092, 313/763-2281, fax 313/764-2475, e-mail: elenhart@umich.edu, for $15 each plus $4.00 postage and handling. Current issue is $30.00 plus $4.00 postage and handling (U.S. funds); $36 (postage & handling included) outside U.S. Annual report usually published in the summer.

Chief Officers of State Library Agencies. *COSLA State Library Agencies Salary Data*. Lexington, KY.

A state-by-state comparative listing of chief officer and staff salary data as of August 31, 1995, including a schedule for updates and revisions to salary ranges. Available for $15, order from COSLA, 167 W. Main St., Suite 600, Lexington, KY 40507, 606/231-1905, fax 606/231-1928.

College and University Personnel Association. *1995-96 National Faculty Salary Survey by Discipline and Rank in Private Four-Year Colleges and Universities*. Washington, D.C.: CUPA.

College and University Personnel Association. *1995-96 National Faculty Salary Survey by Discipline and Rank in Public Four-Year Colleges and Universities.* Washington, D.C.: CUPA.

Annual surveys collect data for five faculty ranks in 55 disciplines and major fields. A total of 500 private and 270 public institutions participated in the most recent study. Communications, Communication Technologies, Computer Information Sciences, and Library Sciences are included. The listings are for those who teach in library science programs, not those who hold faculty rank as academic librarians. Faculty Salary Surveys are each $33 for survey participants, $55 nonpaticipant, CUPA members; and $80 for nonparticipants, nonmembers from CUPA, 1233 20th St., NW, Suite 301, Washington, D.C. 20036, 202/429-0311.

Zipkowitz, Fay. "Placements and Salaries." *Library Journal*.

Annual survey since 1951 of recent graduates of ALA-accredited library and information studies education programs (usually published in a fall issue of *Library Journal* with data from previous calendar year.) For each reporting school, the low, high, average and median salaries are reported for men, women, and total placements. This information is also provided for five regions of the U.S. An additional table shows the distribution of high, low, average and median salaries by type of library for men, women and total placements. The latest listing, "Placements and Salaries 1994" was published in *Library Journal*, October 15, 1995 (pp. 26-33). Canadian schools are no longer included.

Employee Benefits

Although some states collect data on employee benefits, little information is collected on a regional or national level on a regular basis for library workers.

Association of Research Libraries. Office of Management Services. *Benefits for Professional Staff in ARL Libraries.* SPEC Kit 197. Washington, D.C.: ARL, 1993.

Results of a survey of benefits provided by ARL member institutions in 1993 are reported. Information on availability of health care and life insurance, retirement benefits, leave policies, and other perequisites are summarized. Sample policies from ARL libraries are included. Order from ARL/OMS, 21 DuPont Circle, NW, Washington, D.C. 20036, 202/296-8656. $25 (ARL member) or $40 (nonmember) plus $5 s/h per publication.

PROVIDENCE CENTER for Consulting & Planning. *Public Library Work Benefits Survey*. Denton, Tex.: 1996.

Results of a survey of 75 public libraries in 19965 provides salary ranges and average salaries for 5 staff levels, plus data on vacation days, holidays, sick leave, leave of absence, pension plans, health and life insurance, and other benefits. Single copies available for $27.50 plus $2.50 postage/handling, from PROVIDENCE CENTER for Planning & Consulting, PO Box 425979, Denton, TX 76204-5979, 817/898-0300, fax 817/898-0201.

Salary Surveys for Other Library Workers and Related Information Professionals

For salary data on other types of workers that may be employed in libraries, the following surveys might be useful:

Abbott, Langer and Associates, 548 First St., Crete, IL 60417.

Conducts annual or biennial salary surveys for the following fields: legal and related jobs in business and industry; industrial engineers; plant and facilities managers and engineers; consulting engineering firms; consulting firms; geologists; human resources/personnel department; service department; nonprofit organizations; research and development; manufacturing; food and beverage processing; security/loss prevention dept.; MIS/data processing; accounting/financial jobs; advertising agencies; sales/marketing management; and inter-city wage and salary differentials.

The *Compensation in Nonprofit Organizations* report contains information on salaries of Directors of Information with this type of employer. Mean, median, 1st & 3rd quartile, and 1st & 9th decile data, salary ranges, current salaries, and total compensation (salaries plus bonuses) are reported by supervisory responsibility, type of nonprofit organization, total annual budget, geographic scope of organization, number of employees, region, state, and metropolitan area.

Annotations of over 1,200 salary surveys, both domestic and foreign, can be found in *Available Pay Survey Reports: An Annotated Bibliography* (4th ed.) by Dr. Steven Langer (1995). Annotations are indexed by source, geographic area, type of employer, and job title/function/college curricula.

The AMS Foundation, 550 W. Jackson Blvd., Ste. 360, Chicago, IL 60661, 312/236-1840.

Conducts annual surveys of office clerical, secretarial/administrative, professional, data processing and middle management jobs as well as pertinent business trends. The 50th edition of the *Office Clerical, Secretarial/Administrative, Professional, Data Processing and Management Survey* sells for $350; *Contract Labor, Flexible Work, Business Expenses and New Benefits* sell for $30 each.

Datamation publishes an annual salary survey of computer and information systems personnel. The 1995 report will be in the October 1, 1995 issue. This reports on average salaries for positions in systems analysis, programming, database administration, data entry, office automation, and computer operations, by industry and regions.

U.S. Department of Labor, Bureau of Labor Statistics Occupational Compensation Survey Program (OCSP) describes the level and distribution of pay for selected work levels of white-collar and blue-collar occupations nationwide and in a variety of the nation's local labor markets using a consistent survey approach. The program also provides information on the incidence of employee benefits among and within local labor markets.

OCSP compensation data is published for approximately 168 areas. The 'full job list' used for 32 of the larger areas, is comprised of 44 occupations; 4 professional, 9 administrative, 4 technical, 8 clerical, 3 protective service, 8 maintenance and toolroom, and 8 material movement and custodial. The remaining areas are limited to 28 occupations, 202/606-7828, internet: http://stats.bls.gov/ocshome.him.

Appendix B

ALA Policies Relating to Salary Issues

The following are policies endorsed by the ALA Council and included in the "ALA Policy Manual" which appears annually in the *ALA Handbook of Organization*.

Policy #54.1 Library Education and Personnel Utilization

Sec. 8 The title "Librarian" carries with it the connotation of "professional" in the sense that professional tasks are those which require a special background and education on the basis of which library needs are identified, problems are analyzed, goals are set, and original and creative solutions are formulated for them, integrating theory into practice, and planning, organizing, communicating, and administering successful programs of service to users of the library's materials and services. In defining services to users, the professional person recognizes potential users as well as current ones, and designs services which will reach all who could benefit from them.

Sec. 9 The title "Librarian" therefore should be used only to designate positions in libraries which utilize the qualifications and impose the responsibilities suggested above. Positions which are primarily devoted to the routine application of established rules and techniques, however useful and essential to the effective operation of a library's ongoing services, should not carry the word "Librarian" in the job title.

Sec. 11 The salaries for each (personnel) category should offer a range of promotional steps sufficient to permit a career-in-rank. The top salary in any category should overlap the beginning salary in the next higher category, in order to give recognition to the value of experience and knowledge gained on the job.

Sec. 19 Administrative responsibilities entail advanced knowledge and skills comparable to those represented by any other high-level specialty, and appointment to positions in top administration should normally require the qualifications of a Senior Librarian with a specialization in administration. This category, however, is not limited to administrators, whose specialty is only one of several specializations of value to the library service. There are many areas of special knowledge within librarianship which are equally important and to which equal recognition in prestige and salary should be given. Highly qualified persons with specialist responsibilities in some aspects of librarianship--archives, bibliography, reference, for example--should be eligible for advanced status and financial rewards without being forced to abandon for administrative responsibilities their areas of major competence.

Policy #54.4 Comparable Rewards

The American Library Association supports salary administration which gives reasonable and comparable recognition to positions having administrative, technical, subject, and linguistic requirements. It is recognized that all such specialist competencies can be intellectually vigorous and meet demanding professional operational needs. In administering such a policy, it can be a useful guide that, in major libraries, as many nonadministrative specialties be assigned to the top classifications as are administrative staff. Whenever possible there should be as many at the top rank with less than 30 percent administrative load as there are at the highest rank carrying over 70 percent administrative load.

Policy #54.7 Security of Employment for Library Employees

Security of employment, as an elementary right, guarantees specifically.....a sufficient degree of economic security to make employment in the library attractive to men and women of ability.

Policy #54.8 The Library's Pay Plan

Libraries should have a well-constructed and well-administered pay plan based on systematic analysis and evaluation of jobs in the library and which will assure equal pay for equal work. (Note: For text of full statement, see section following listing of policies.)

Policy #54.9 Permanent Part-Time Employment

The right to earn a living includes a right to part-time employment on a par with full-time employment, including prorated pay and fringe benefits, opportunity for advancement and protection of tenure, access to middle and upper level jobs, and exercise of full responsibilities at any level.

ALA shall create more voluntarily chosen upgraded permanent part-time jobs in its own organization and supports similar action on the part of all libraries.

Policy #54.10 Equal Opportunity and Salaries

The American Library Association supports and works for the achievement of equal salaries and opportunity for employment and promotion for men and women.

The Association fully supports the concept of comparable wages for comparable work that aims at levels of pay for female-oriented occupations equal to those of male-oriented occupations; ALA therefore supports all legal and legislative efforts to achieve wages for library workers commensurate with wages in other occupations with similar qualifications, training, and responsibilities.

ALA particularly supports the efforts of those library workers who have documented, and are legally challenging, the practice of discriminatory salaries, and whose success will benefit all library workers throughout the nation.

Policy #54.11 Collective Bargaining

The American Library Association recognizes the principle of collective bargaining as one of the methods of conducting labor-management relations used by private and public institutions. The Association affirms the right of eligible library employees to organize and bargain collectively with their employers, or to refrain from organizing and bargaining collectively, without fear of reprisal.

Policy #54.18 Advertising Salary Ranges

Available ranges shall be given for positions listed in any placement services provided by ALA and its units. A regional salary guide delineating the latest minimum salary figures recommended by state library associations shall be made available from any placement services provided by ALA and its units.

All ALA and unit publications printing classified job advertisements shall list the salary ranges established for open positions where available and shall include a regional salary guide delineating the latest minimum salary figures recommended by state library associations for library positions.

Full Text of Policy # 54.8: The Library's Pay Plan*

The American Library Association believes that an important factor in establishing and maintaining good library service is adequate pay for library employees as exemplified in a well-constructed and well-administered pay plan. A knowledge of the principles on which sound salary administration is based must be the foundation of an equitable pay plan. To aid the library's governing board, its administration, and its staff in the formulation, promulgation, and operation of such a pay plan, the
ALA Board on Personnel Administration sets forth in a series of related statements the principles of salary planning and administration.

1. A sound pay plan will be predicated on a systematic analysis and evaluation of jobs in the library, and will reflect the current organization and objectives of the library, recognizing different levels of difficulty and responsibility inherent in various positions, whether these are classified as professional, nonprofessional, administrative, specialist, maintenance, or trade; the relationship among positions in terms of difficulty and responsibility will thus be expressed in a unified plan which will integrate all types of service and will assure equal pay for equal work.

2. An equitable salary schedule will be provided for each class of position which is comparable to that received by persons employed in analogous work in the area and required to have analogous training and qualifications.

    The salaries of nonprofessional employees, maintenance and skilled trade workers employed by the library system will compare with those of local workers performing similar duties. The salary schedules for professional library positions, in the case of the community where the pay scale does not meet competing rates outside, may need to exceed the prevailing local level for other professional personnel. Since the recruiting of professionally trained librarians is on a nation-wide basis, the library system must compete with rates paid in the country as a whole in order to obtain and retain a high quality of professional personnel. In libraries in educational institutions (elementary, secondary, and higher education) the professional librarians will normally be on the faculty pay plan, with the salary schedules of the various classes of faculty rank adjusted to compensate equitably for such factors as shorter vacations and longer work week; where a separate pay plan is used, it will be comparable with that of the faculty and adjusted to compensate equitably for such factors as vacation and work week.

3. An equitable salary schedule will provide for each class of position a minimum and a maximum salary and a series of increments within each salary range, such increments to be granted on the basis of demonstrated competence, individual development (whether through growth on the job or through formal education), and attitude.

*Note: This policy was passed by the ALA Council in July 1955. It still remains a useful statement regarding the administration of a library's pay plan. Readers should note, however, that the references to the Board on Personnel Administration are not applicable since this unit is no longer in existence.

4. The library system in developing a pay plan, and in reviewing it to maintain its adequacy, will identify one or more key positions in the professional and in the other services, set salary schedules for these positions which are comparable to prevailing rates for such positions, and develop and adjust the salary schedule for other levels of positions in relation to the salary schedules set for each of these key positions.

5. The pay plan ladder consisting of the salary schedules for the various classes of positions will provide an

orderly progression from the lowest to the highest schedule, with each schedule reflecting properly the difference in level of duties and responsibilities of positions in that classification from those in the schedule below and above it but without wide gaps or serious overlapping between schedules.

6. An equitable pay plan will reflect living costs in the community, the cost of maintaining an appropriate level of living, and the ability of the jurisdiction to pay for the service.

7. All policies and rules concerning the operation and administration of the pay plan will be set forth clearly in writing and will accompany the pay plan.

8. Though final approval and adoption of the pay plan and rules for its operation rest with the governing board and administration of the library, it is desirable that the library staff participates in the formulation of both the plan and its operating rules.

9. Each staff member will be informed of the salary schedule for his or her class of position, of the relation of that schedule to the pay plan as a whole, and of the policies and rules governing the operation of the plan.

The current studies of the ALA Board on Personnel Administration giving salary data for key positions will provide useful material for the library system in developing and maintaining the adequacy of its pay plan.

Appendix C

Selected Bibliography on Compensation and Employee Benefits

Compiled by the
ALA Library and Research Center

Note: The earlier editions of *ALA Survey of Librarian Salaries* contained selected citations on compensation that readers may wish to consult since many of these references are still useful. Items listed below have been published since the previous listings were compiled.

Beatty, Kate L. "Pay and Benefits Break Away from Tradition." *HRMagazine* 39:63+ (November 1994).

Bennett, Linda. "Compensation Fads, Custom Pay Plans, and Team Pay." *Compensation & Benefits Review* 28:67-75 (March/April 1996).

Grib, Gail and Susan O'Donnell. "Pay Plans that Reward Employee Achievement." *HRMagazine* 40:49+ (July 1995).

Lawler, Edward E., III. "The New Pay: A Strategic Approach." *Compensation & Benefits Review* 27:14-22 (July/August 1995).

Ledford, Gerald E., Jr. "Paying for the Skills, Knowledge, and Competencies of Knowledge Workers." *Compensation & Benefits Review* 27:55-62 (July/August 1995).

Leonard, Bill. "New Ways to Pay Employees." *HRMagazine* 39:61+ (February 1994).

Lissy, William E. and Marlene L. Morgenstern. "Currents in Compensation and Benefits." *Compensation & Benefits Review* 27:15-25 (November/December 1995).

Mazmanian, Adam. "Big Salary Gains for Special Librarians (SLA Salary Survey)." *Library Journal* 121:20 (February 1, 1996).

Mitra, Atul, et al. "The Case of the Invisible Merit Raise: How People See Their Pay Raises." *Compensation & Benefits Review* 27:71-76 (May/June 1995).

Morgenstern, Marlene L. "Salary and Wage." *Compensation & Benefits Review*. 28:6-9 (May/June 1996).

"Salaries of Public Library Directors." *Library Personnel News* 9:6 (May/June 1995).

Vogeley, Edward G., and Louise J. Schaeffer. "Link Employee Pay to Competencies and Objectives." *HRMagazine* 40:75+ (October 1995).

Zipkowitz, Fay. "New Directions for Recent Grads (Placements and Salaries 1994)." *Library Journal* 120:26-33 (October 15, 1995).

Appendix D

Technical Considerations

Formation of Library Groups

As in previous years, the survey samples were selected from two library universes--public and academic. The public library universe included all public libraries serving populations of 25,000 or more and was stratified into two classes--those serving populations of from 25,000 to 99,999 and those serving populations of 100,000 or more.

The academic library universe was stratified into three classes: two-year college, four-year college, and university. This stratification was based on the "Highest Offering" code used in the *1995 Higher Education Directory* published by Higher Education Publications, Inc. The first of these three classes include schools that offer "two but less than four years." The second includes schools that offer a "four or five year baccalaureate." The third combines four categories: "first professional degree," "master's," "beyond master's but less than doctorate," "doctorate."

Within each of these five strata, libraries were further stratified into four geographic areas used frequently by National Center for Education Statistics (NCES): North Atlantic, Great Lakes and Plains, Southeast, and West and Southwest. A list of states included in each region is provided in Table D-1. As in previous surveys, the five library classes and four geographic areas were combined to form twenty groups from which samples were selected. Tables D2-D7 show the size of each group, the size of the sample, and the size of the return.

Sample Selection and Return

The size of the sample for each type/size/geographic strata was determined by using a proportional sampling procedure that took into account the size of the population in each group and the expected return rate for the survey. As has been done since 1992, the public library sample was selected using a diskette from the NCES containing data on all public libraries submitted to NCES by state library agencies as part of the Federal State Cooperative System for Public Library Data (FSCS). This file includes data on the number of staff with master's degrees from programs in library and information studies accredited by ALA. Before selecting the sample, we dropped from the sampling frame libraries that did not have at least two of such personnel. Once the sampling frame was established, the sample was drawn by strata as described above.

The procedure for selecting the academic library sample was similar to the procedure followed since 1994. The Library Research Center (LRC) used a sampling frame from John Minter Associates based on the *1996 Higher Education Directory* and a diskette from NCES on "Academic Libraries, 1992." LRC screened out several sets of institutions from the full universe. Removed were institutions with fewer than two full-time professionals and institutions categorized as "specialized" by the Carnegie Corporation for the Advancement of Teaching. Those institutions offer degrees ranging from the bachelor's to the doctorate, at least 50 percent of which are in a single specialized field, e.g., "theological seminaries, Bible colleges, and other institutions offering degrees in religion," and "Schools of art, music, and design." Specialized institutions often declined to respond in the early years of this survey. Also excluded were four sets of institutions whose individual members had been unable to respond in the past. In New York, the seventeen institutions that are part of the City University of New York were removed because librarians there have full academic status and salary is not related to position description. Public two-year schools in California were removed for the same reason as were the fourteen members of the state university system in Pennsylvania. Also in Pennsylvania, we removed all but the main campus of Pennsylvania State University because librarians at other campuses declined to respond in the past and referred us to the main campus. The remaining institutions were sampled using the stratification plan described above. Finally, the preliminary sample was screened for libraries that refused to respond in the years from 1990 through 1995 for reasons that seemed unlikely to change. Five such libraries were dropped from the sample.

In addition to the 966 returns analyzed for this report, we also received 24 returns that could not be used. They fell into the following categories:

- three were from respondents in libraries where none of the staff are full-time or none of the full-time staff had master's degrees from programs in library and information studies accredited by ALA.

- six were refusals. All were from academic libraries. In two cases the librarian does not have access to staff salary data.

- three were blank.

- seven were unusable for miscellaneous reasons (e.g., incomplete data, salaries not related to position).

- four arrived too late

- one was public library system that primarily serves other libraries. Questionnaires had been sent because of a flaw in the sampling frame.

Procedure

The questionnaire and cover letter were mailed on March 31, 1996. A postage-paid business reply envelope was enclosed to encourage response. A second mailing was sent to all non-respondents in April. A third mailing was sent in May only to non-respondents in several strata where response was under 70 percent.

Questionnaires were returned to the Library Research Center (LRC) of the University of Illinois Graduate School of Library and Information Science, where they were edited, entered into a microcomputer file, and analyzed using SPSS for Windows.

Again this year a special procedure was followed for libraries that are members of the Association of Research Libraries. ARL, which includes about 100 of the largest university libraries in the U.S., conducts its own annual salary survey. Data are gathered for salaries as of July 1 and published the following spring. ARL libraries are also included in the sample for the ALA survey. In the past, some have declined to answer because they are unable to spend time completing another salary questionnaire. For the 1996 survey, ARL again agreed to cooperate with us to save work for everyone. After the sample was selected, we identified the ARL libraries on the list and sent the directors a special mailing asking them to release salaries already on file with ARL. Twenty-one of the twenty-three ARL libraries in the sample agreed to release data. We sent ARL a list of the ARL position codes that matched the position descriptions in our questionnaire and ARL sent salary data on electronically for those positions in the selected institutions. These salaries were entered into the data file along with salaries from other libraries.

This procedure worked well and saved time both in the libraries involved and in survey processing. It has two drawbacks, however. ARL salary figures are as of July 1995 whereas others are as of the following April. Thus, the figures for salaries in the university category in our report may be lower than what was paid in April 1996. Also, ARL does not specify that salaries should be reported only for staff with master's degrees from programs in library and information studies accredited by ALA and some ARL libraries include "other professionals" as well as librarians. For the most part, however, we expect that those "other professionals" are in the ARL position code of "Functional Specialist" which was *not* on the list of codes we requested from ARL. On balance, we believe this procedure had more benefits than drawbacks and intend to continue it as long as ARL is willing to cooperate.

Table D-1. States in Four Regions of the U.S.

NORTH ATLANTIC	GREAT LAKES AND PLAINS	SOUTHEAST	WEST AND SOUTHWEST
Connecticut	Illinois	Alabama	Alaska
Delaware	Indiana	Arkansas	Arizona
District of Columbia	Iowa	Florida	California
Maine	Kansas	Georgia	Colorado
Maryland	Michigan	Kentucky	Hawaii
Massachusetts	Minnesota	Louisiana	Idaho
New Hampshire	Missouri	Mississippi	Montana
New Jersey	Nebraska	North Carolina	Nevada
New York	North Dakota	South Carolina	New Mexico
Pennsylvania	Ohio	Tennessee	Oklahoma
Rhode Island	South Dakota	Virginia	Oregon
Vermont	Wisconsin	West Virginia	Texas
			Utah
			Washington
			Wyoming

Source: *Statistics of Public Libraries, 1977-78* (NCES, 1982)

Table D-2. Medium-Sized Public Libraries: Size of Group, Sample, Return

	GROUP	SAMPLE		RETURN	
	#	#	% of Group	#	% of Sample
North Atlantic	315	126	40.0	95	75.4
Great Lakes & Plains	299	120	40.1	96	80.0
Southeast	174	70	40.2	51	72.9
West and Southwest	176	71	40.3	58	81.7
TOTAL	964	387	40.1	300	77.5

Table D-3. Large Public Libraries: Size of Group, Sample, Return

	GROUP	SAMPLE		RETURN	
	#	#	% of Group	#	% of Sample
North Atlantic	63	46	73.0	34	73.9
Great Lakes & Plains	90	46	51.1	36	78.3
Southeast	133	62	46.6	49	79.0
West and Southwest	147	76	51.7	59	77.6
TOTAL	433	230	53.1	178	77.4

Table D-4. Two-Year College Libraries: Size of Group, Sample, Return

	GROUP	SAMPLE		RETURN	
	#	#	% of Group	#	% of Sample
North Atlantic	127	46	36.2	34	73.9
Great Lakes & Plains	114	46	40.4	34	73.9
Southeast	163	56	34.4	40	71.4
West and Southwest	126	46	36.5	38	82.6
TOTAL	530	194	36.6	146	75.3

Table D-5. Four-Year College Libraries: Size of Group, Sample, Return

	GROUP	SAMPLE		RETURN	
	#	#	% of Group	#	% of Sample
North Atlantic	86	46	53.5	33	71.7
Great Lakes & Plains	111	46	41.4	33	71.7
Southeast	101	46	45.5	32	69.6
West and Southwest	27	26	96.3	18	69.2
TOTAL	325	164	50.5	116	70.7

Table D-6. University Libraries: Size of Group, Sample, Return

	GROUP	SAMPLE		RETURN	
	#	#	% of Group	#	% of Sample
North Atlantic	246	85	34.6	63	74.1
Great Lakes & Plains	217	75	34.6	57	76.0
Southeast	203	70	34.5	52	74.3
West and Southwest	211	73	34.6	54	74.0
TOTAL	877	303	34.5	226	74.6

Table D-7. All Libraries Surveyed: Size of Group, Sample, Return

	GROUP	SAMPLE		RETURN	
	#	#	% of Group	#	% of Sample
North Atlantic	837	349	41.7	259	74.2
Great Lakes & Plains	831	333	40.1	256	76.9
Southeast	774	304	39.3	224	73.7
West and Southwest	687	292	42.5	227	77.7
TOTAL	3,129	1,278	40.8	966	75.6

50 East Huron Street
Chicago, Illinois 60611-2795
USA

Telephone 312 944 6780
Fax 312 440 9374
TDD 312 944 7298
E-mail:ala@ala.org
http://www.ala.org

Appendix E

ALAAmericanLibraryAssociation

Dear Colleague: March 31, 1996

ALA needs your help in providing information to the library community. The enclosed survey concerns salaries paid to librarians with master's degrees from programs in library and information studies accredited by ALA who hold full-time positions in academic and public libraries. Your institution has been selected as part of a random sample of libraries to receive the enclosed questionnaire. Only summary results will be reported; individual responses will not be identified.

ALA collected and published similar information biennially from 1982 to 1988, and annually since 1989. The results of these surveys have been useful to many people in the library community who need to know what salary might be paid to someone in a particular type of library position or in a particular geographical area. This information is useful to librarians applying for positions, to librarians setting salaries, and to many others interested in the compensation of librarians.

Because your library is one of a scientifically selected sample, your response is essential to the success of the survey. As an indication of our thanks for your help, all participants are entitled to a 25% discount on the price of the report. (Mention this entitlement when you place an order. The report will be published in September, 1996.) If your staff is very large and this form is difficult to use, please contact Mary Jo Lynch at one of the numbers given below. We want your response and will work with you to make use of whatever data you can provide.

Please complete the questionnaire and return it in the enclosed self-addressed, postage-paid envelope. Please return it as soon as possible, but no later than **April 16, 1996**. If you have questions about the survey, please contact Mary Jo Lynch, Director, ALA Office for Research and Statistics at 1-800-545-2433, extension 4273; mjlynch@ala.org (Internet).

Thank you very much for your cooperation.

Sincerely yours,

Elizabeth Martinez
Executive Director
American Library Association

EM/kd

Enclosures (2)

P.S. Please help our budget by returning this form promptly. In order to ensure the validity of the results, reminders will be sent to nonrespondents. However, we would rather spend the postage money on other services.

Appendix F

AMERICAN LIBRARY ASSOCIATION SURVEY OF LIBRARIAN SALARIES, 1996

PART I. SALARIES PAID TO BEGINNING LIBRARIANS

A. Within the last 12 months has the library hired any full-time staff with master's degrees from programs in library and information studies accredited by ALA but no professional experience? Circle one

No (if so, skip to Part II) 1
Yes 2

B. What is the annual salary paid such staff? Please list all annual salaries below as of April 1, 1996. **Do not repeat salaries of these librarians in Part II**. NOTE FOR ACADEMIC LIBRARIES: If the incumbent works LESS than a 12-month year (including vacation), please report the salary and circle the appropriate number of months (9 or 10) for which the salary is paid.

Annual Salary	Annual Salary	Annual Salary	Annual Salary
1 _____ 9 10	3 _____ 9 10	5 _____ 9 10	7 _____ 9 10
2 _____ 9 10	4 _____ 9 10	6 _____ 9 10	8 _____ 9 10

PART II. SALARIES PAID TO LIBRARIANS IN SELECTED POSITIONS

This section of the questionnaire requests information on annual salaries for selected positions ordinarily held by full-time staff with master's degrees from programs in library and information studies accredited by ALA.

We realize that many libraries have positions that are not included in the questionnaire. **Do not include salaries for those positions**. Libraries may also fill the positions listed here with staff who have credentials other than master's degrees from programs accredited by ALA. **Do not include salaries for those staff. Also, do not include salaries for part-time or support staff.**

Each page in Part II contains descriptions of several specific library positions. If your library has one or more staff with the specified degree employed **FULL-TIME** whose major responsibilities are covered by the position description, please provide the information requested on the form unless the salary was listed above in Part I, B. If a staff member works full-time but performs duties of more than one position, list him or her as incumbent in the position that you consider his or her major responsibility. **List each staff member only once** and give the full salary paid to the person. All **FULL-TIME** incumbents in these positions should be included regardless of the number of months worked in a year.* NOTE FOR ACADEMIC LIBRARIES: If the incumbent is considered full-time but works LESS than a 12-month year (including vacation), please report the salary and circle the appropriate number of months (9 or 10) for which the salary is paid.

For each position in which you have staff with master's degrees from programs in library and information studies accredited by ALA employed **FULL-TIME**, please provide the annual salary of each incumbent as of April 1, 1996 except for the beginning librarians reported above in Part I, B. Give actual dollars paid. Do not include fringe benefits. If you need additional space, please use separate sheets of paper or attach a computer printout.

*If services are contributed (i.e., institution pays some expenses or an honorarium but not a true salary), please do not list the incumbent.

POSITION TITLE: *Director* *

POSITION DESCRIPTION: *Chief administrative officer of the library or library system. Plans and directs all aspects of the operation. May have job title such as Librarian or Head Librarian.*

POSITION TITLE: *(if different from above)*

ANNUAL SALARY _____ 9 10

Note for academic libraries: Circle 9 or 10 as appropriate if salary is for LESS than a 12 month year (including vacation).

POSITION TITLE: *Deputy/Associate/Assistant Director* *

POSITION DESCRIPTION: *Aids Director in planning and directing some or all aspects of library or library system. May manage a major aspect of the library operation (e.g., technical services, public services, collection development, systems/automation).*

POSITION TITLE: *(if different from above)* _____

Annual Salary	Annual Salary	Annual Salary	Annual Salary
1 _____ 9 10	3 _____ 9 10	5 _____ 9 10	7 _____ 9 10
2 _____ 9 10	4 _____ 9 10	6 _____ 9 10	8 _____ 9 10

POSITION TITLE: *Department Head/Branch Head* *

POSITION DESCRIPTION: *Manages operation of a library unit that is physically separate from the main library (e.g., a branch or a department library) or of one aspect of the main library (e.g., Reference Department, Serials Department, Children's Department).*

POSITION TITLE: *(if different from above)* _____

Annual Salary	Annual Salary	Annual Salary	Annual Salary
1 _____ 9 10	5 _____ 9 10	9 _____ 9 10	13 _____ 9 10
2 _____ 9 10	6 _____ 9 10	10 _____ 9 10	14 _____ 9 10
3 _____ 9 10	7 _____ 9 10	11 _____ 9 10	15 _____ 9 10
4 _____ 9 10	8 _____ 9 10	12 _____ 9 10	16 _____ 9 10

---

* Report only full-time staff *with master's degrees from programs in library and information studies accredited by ALA.* Do not repeat salaries reported in Part I.

POSITION TITLE: *Reference/Information Librarian* *

POSITION DESCRIPTION: *Locates information for library users or helps users find it in print or electronic sources. Answers questions and gives instruction about the use of sources in the library or available electronically. Makes decisions about acquiring sources or arranging for access to them.*

POSITION TITLE: *(if different from above)* _____

Annual Salary	Annual Salary	Annual Salary	Annual Salary
1 _____9/10	4 _____9/10	7 _____9/10	10 _____9/10
2 _____9/10	5 _____9/10	8 _____9/10	11 _____9/10
3 _____9/10	6 _____9/10	9 _____9/10	12 _____9/10

POSITION TITLE: *Cataloger and/or Classifier* *

POSITION DESCRIPTION: *Organizes all types of material purchased by the library. Describes each item in standard format and assigns access points. Assigns subject headings and classification numbers. Uses automated systems. May be involved with only descriptive cataloging or only subject cataloging/classification.*

POSITION TITLE: *(if different from above)* _____

Annual Salary	Annual Salary	Annual Salary	Annual Salary
1 _____9/10	3 _____9/10	5 _____9/10	7 _____9/10
2 _____9/10	4 _____9/10	6 _____9/10	8 _____9/10

POSITION TITLE: *Children's and/or Young Adult Services Librarian* *

POSITION DESCRIPTION: *Plans and conducts library services for children and/or young adults. Advises on reading materials. Selects materials for the collection. May plan and conduct special programs and outreach services.*

POSITION TITLE: *(if different from above)* _____

Annual Salary	Annual Salary	Annual Salary	Annual Salary
1 _____9/10	3 _____9/10	5 _____9/10	7 _____9/10
2 _____9/10	4 _____9/10	6 _____9/10	8 _____9/10

* Report only full-time staff *with master's degrees from programs in library and information studies accredited by ALA.* Do not repeat salaries reported in Part I.

PART III. SUPPLEMENTARY QUESTIONS

Your answer to these questions will help us improve the way ALA provides salary information.

1a. Does your library have the *ALA Survey of Libraries Salaries, 1995*?

    ____ Yes (Skip to 2a)
    ____ No
    ____ Don't Know (Skip to 3)

1b. Why do you not have a copy? (Check all that apply and skip to 3)

    ____ Did not know about it
    ____ Can't afford it
    ____ Don't need it

2a. Have you used a copy in the last twelve months?

    ____ Yes
    ____ No (Skip to 3)

2b. How did it help you? (Check all that apply)

    ____ Setting salaries for a new position
    ____ Bargaining for increase in salary for my staff
    ____ Bargaining for increase in salary for myself
    ____ Other (please specify)

3. Please comment on how ALA could provide more useful information on librarian salaries.

A. Name and title of respondent **: _____

B. Telephone number: ( ) _____

** *Neither libraries nor individuals will be identified in the report of this survey. The name of your library is given here so that we can avoid sending reminders to libraries who respond. The name and phone number of the person responding are requested because we may need to contact him or her if we have questions about this return.*

*THANK YOU VERY MUCH! Please return by **April 16, 1996** in the enclosed postage paid envelope to:*
    Library Research Center
    University of Illinois at Urbana-Champaign
    501 East Daniel Street
    Champaign, Illinois 61820

PLACE LABEL HERE

Appendix G

Salaries Paid for Less Than a Twelve Month Year in Academic Libraries

Instructions on the questionnaire told the respondent: If the incumbent works **less** than a 12-month year (including vacation), please report the salary and circle the appropriate number of months (9 or 10) for which the salary is paid.

A program was written to prorate these salaries to their twelve month equivalents for the purpose of reporting results of this survey. Table G was created to show how often this process was necessary. The first column shows the total number of incumbents for which salaries are reported in each of the three types of academic institutions on the position tables in this report. The second column shows how many were reported as being for nine months and the third column shows the percentage of incumbents in the category (position/type of library) which that number represents. The following columns repeat that pattern for positions reported as being for ten months and then for a combination of nine and ten month salaries.

Table G.

Salaries Paid for Less Than a 12-month Year in Academic Libraries by Position and Type

POSITION AND TYPE OF LIBRARY	ALL INCUMBENTS #	9-MONTH #	9-MONTH %	10-MONTH #	10-MONTH %	9 AND 10 MONTH #	9 AND 10 MONTH %
Director							
Two-year college	131	7	5	11	8	17	13
Four-year college	113	4	4	4	4	8	8
University	216			4	2	4	2
Deputy/Associate/Assistant Director							
Two-year college	45	3	7	3	7	6	14
Four-year college	52	1	2	5	10	6	12
University	302	3	1			3	1
Department Head/Branch Head							
Two-year college	59	15	25	9	15	24	40
Four-year college	70	8	11	3	4	11	15
University	965	24	2	14	1	38	3
Reference/Information Librarian							
Two-year college	150	24	16	18	12	42	28
Four-year college	120	8	7	15	13	23	20
University	956	32	3	31	3	63	6
Cataloger and/or Classifier							
Two-year college	56	9	16	6	11	15	27
Four-year college	57	5	9	6	11	11	20
University	465	12	3	11	2	23	5
Beginning Librarian							
Academic, Two Year	26	4	15	3	12	7	27
Academic, Four Year	20	3	15	1	5	4	20
Academic, University	109	1	1	3	3	4	4